The author wishes to thank the following persons
whose efforts made this book possible.

Hester Callahan

Phoebe MacAdams

Maxcy Callahan

A FONDUE PARTY IS A FUN AND EASY WAY TO ENTERTAIN!

You can have a perfect get-together everytime with this unique book.

● This is the most complete book available on fondue. It contains a wide variety of meat and cheese fondue recipes plus special desserts, baked fondues, rarebits, and more.

● With this book, a fondue party is more than a feast, it is a "happening" -- it makes for a unique, memorable occasion.

● Complete information about the selection, use and care of fondue equipment is included, as well as instructions on how to get along without it, if necessary.

● As with all Nitty Gritty Cookbooks, the recipes are easy to follow and are printed one per page in large, easy - to - read type.

● For added convenience, this book is uniquely designed to take a minimum of counter space and to keep your place when pressed open.

SATISFACTION GUARANTEE – If you are not completely satisfied with any Nitty Gritty book, we will gladly refund your purchase price. Simply return it to us within 30 days along with your receipt.

the FONDUE cookbook

by Ed Callahan

Illustrations by Howard Sanders

A Nitty Gritty Book*
Published by
Nitty Gritty Productions
P.O. Box 5457
Concord, California 94524

*Nitty Gritty Books - Trademark
Owned by Nitty Gritty Productions
Concord, California

ISBN 0-911954-01-5

Library of Congress Catalog Card Number: 77-670103

TABLE OF CONTENTS

INTRODUCTION

Fondue isn't just a delicious feast, it is a social event, and the camaradierie which it inspires makes it unique.

The peasant custom of everyone eating out of the same pot is not new. But in Switzerland, this custom was combined with a goodly amount of inventiveness to create a "happening" which has become a world-wide favorite. Friends everywhere are spending pleasant hours together preparing and enjoying fondues of all kinds.

Although the word fondue comes from the French word *fondre*, meaning *to melt*, the name has taken on a broader connotation and now popularly implies not just the dish itself, but the entire ritual which surrounds it.

From the original cheese fondue evolved the even more popular Fondue

Bourguignonne, with all of its variations, and then in natural order from this country came dessert fondues. Although baked fondue, which also originated in this country, isn't at all similar to either the classic Swiss Fondue or Fondue Bourguignonne, it is a popular make-ahead party dish and we have chosen to include it in our collection of fondues. Rarebits, on the other hand, bear no similarity of name but are quite like many of the cheese fondues. They can even be served with bread cubes for dipping as well as spooned over toast, or what have you, in the traditional manner.

The classic-type cheese fondues can be prepared in an earthenware pot called a caquelon, or a metal pot designed primarily for Fondue Bourguignonne, or a chafing dish. Some fondue mixtures and rarebits do not stand up well over direct heat, and so they must be prepared and served over hot water. Because a chafing dish can be used in much the same way as a double boiler, it is by far the best to use under these circumstances. The various pots come in different sizes, shapes and prices. Special fondue forks are not essential but make the dipping process easier and more fun. It really isn't necessary to have special fondue equipment, but inexpensive sets are readily available and the more decorative the pot and other elements, the more festive the effect.

Fondue parties are innovative events. You may serve what you wish as long as the basic ingredients—good friends and a communal pot—are there. The popularity of these parties is understandable since they offer a maximum of fun with a minimum of effort. An evening spent with friends enjoying the pleasures of the fondue pot and lively conversation is always memorable.

LA FONDUE—CLASSIC AND OTHERWISE

It is no surprise that the two major elements in Switzerland's national dish are cheese and bread, since both have long been important parts of the Swiss diet. It is supposed that the whole thing came about when cheese and bread, which were made in the summer to be eaten during the long winter months, became extremely hard and dry, but not inedible. It was discovered that the cheese became tasty again if melted and the hard pieces of bread, dipped into the bubbly cheese, became soft enough to chew! This ancient discovery is still one of today's favorite culinary delights known as La Fondue. People love to gather around a communal pot to dip bite-size pieces of bread in the delicious combination of cheese melted in wine. Although stale bread is no longer favored, long loaves of French or Italian bread should be cut so that each cube has some crust, and then lightly toasted in the oven.

CLASSIC FONDUE—RECIPE AND RITUAL

1/2 lb. Emmenthaler cheese	1 tbs. lemon juice
1/2 lb. Gruyère cheese	1 tsp. cornstarch
1 clove garlic	3 tbs. Kirsch
2 cups dry white wine	dash nutmeg and paprika

Finely dice or coarsely shred the cheese. It will melt better than if finely grated. Cut garlic in half. Rub fondue pot and wooden spoon with cut side and then discard it. Pour wine into pot. Set over moderate heat. When hot (never boil) add lemon juice. Lightly toss flour and cheese. Drop by handfuls into hot wine. Stir constantly with wooden spoon. Allow each addition to melt before adding the next. Continue stirring in a figure eight motion until cheese is melted. Add Kirsch and spices and serve.

Place the fondue pot in the middle of the table over lowest heat setting. Provide each guest (not more than 4 or 5 to a pot) with a fondue fork and bread cubes. The first person spears a bread cube on the fork and swirls it into the cheese mixture until it is well coated and then eats it. The process is repeated around the table, each person taking his turn in order.

There are various Swiss traditions surrounding the unfortunate person who drops his bread in the fondue pot. A lady must pay her debt by kissing the man nearest her and a man pays by buying the wine; or perhaps it might mean only a loss of one's next turn.

The brown crust which remains in the bottom of the pot should be removed with a knife and divided among the diners. Many people think the crust is the best part of the fondue!

If serving Classic Swiss Fondue as a main course, the rest of the menu might consist of a crisp green salad tossed with raw vegetables and a light oil and fresh lemon juice dressing, chilled white wine and for dessert a fresh fruit tray, baked apples or short cakes topped with fresh or poached fruit.

VARIATIONS

FONDUE VERMOUTH—Use dry vermouth instead of dry white wine.

FONDUE GORGONZOLA ET TILSITER—Use 1/3 gorgonzola, 1/3 tilsiter and 1/3 Gruyère.

CONTINENTAL FONDUE

1 clove garlic, cut in half
1/2 lb. Swiss cheese, minced
1/2 lb. Italian cheese, minced
3/4 cup dry white wine
2 tbs. brandy
French or Italian bread, cubed

Rub bottom and sides of chafing dish or fondue pot with cut garlic. Add cheese and pour wine over it. Let stand at room temperature 4 to 5 hours. A few minutes before serving time, place over low heat. Stir constantly until cheese melts and mixture is smooth. Blend in brandy and seasonings. Eat by spearing bread cubes on forks and dipping into mixture. Makes 4 servings.

FONDUE SONOMA

1 clove garlic, cut in half
2 cups California Riesling wine
1 lb. Swiss cheese, diced
1 tsp. flour
freshly grated pepper
3 tbs. California brandy
French or Italian bread, cubed

Rub inside of fondue pot and wooden spoon with cut garlic. Pour in wine and warm over low heat. Toss cheese with flour. Add to heated wine a little at a time. Stir until melted. Blend in seasonings and brandy. Serve. Eat by spearing bread cubes on forks and dipping into mixture. Makes 6 servings.

FONDUE CHABLIS FOR TWO

1/2 lb. Swiss cheese, minced
1-1/2 tsp. flour
1 clove garlic, cut in half
1/2 cup chablis wine
pinch nutmeg and pepper
French or Italian bread, cubed

Toss cheese with flour. Rub fondue pot and wooden spoon with cut garlic. Pour in wine. Heat, but do not boil. Add cheese. Stir until melted. Add seasonings and serve. Eat by spearing bread on forks and dipping into mixture. Makes 2 generous servings.

FONDUE ROYALE

2 cups champagne
2 truffles, thinly sliced
1 lb. Swiss cheese, diced
1 tsp. flour

2 egg yolks, beaten
truffle liquor
white pepper
French or Italian bread, cubed

Pour 1-2/3 cups champagne into fondue pot. Add truffles. Warm over low heat. Add cheese gradually. Stir until melted. Combine egg yolks, truffles liquor and remaining 1/3 cup champagne. Slowly stir into cheese mixture. Add seasonings. Serve. Eat by spearing bread cubes on forks and dipping into mixture. Makes 6 servings.

EGG FONDUE

1 clove garlic

3/4 cup white wine

2 cups (8 oz.) grated Swiss cheese

2 tbs. butter

6 eggs, beaten

salt and pepper to taste

French or Italian bread, cubed

Press garlic into wine. Pour into saucepan and boil until reduced to half the original volume. In a chafing dish blazer pan, over hot water, combine cheese, eggs and seasonings. Stir until cheese melts and mixture is smooth. Slowly blend reduced wine into cheese mixture and serve. Eat by spearing bread cubes on forks and dipping into mixture. Makes 4 servings.

FONDUE DE BERNE

1 clove garlic, cut in half
1/2 cup dry white wine
1 lb. Emmenthaler cheese, minced
4 egg yolks

1/3 cup cream
pinch nutmeg and paprika
French or Italian bread, cubed

Rub the inside of chafing dish blazer pan with cut garlic. Pour in wine and heat over hot water. Add cheese gradually. Stir constantly until melted. Combine egg yolks, cream and seasonings. Slowly blend into cheese mixture. Cook, stirring, until mixture is thickened and creamy. Eat by spearing bread cubes on forks and dipping into mixture. Makes 6 servings.

FONDUE JEUNE FILLE

1/4 cup butter

2 tbs. flour

1-1/2 cups dry white wine, heated

1 cup (4 oz.) grated Swiss cheese

3 egg yolks

3 tbs. cream

nutmeg, salt and cayenne to taste

French or Italian bread, cubed

Melt butter in fondue pot over moderate heat. Stir in flour and let bubble. Remove from heat. Slowly blend in wine. Return to heat and cook, stirring, until mixture is thickened. Add cheese. Combine egg yolks and cream. Stir into mixture until well blended. Season to taste and serve. Eat by spearing the bread cubes on forks and dipping into mixture. Makes 4 servings.

FONDUTA

From the Piedmont region of Italy which is famous for Fontina cheese and pungent white truffles.

3/4 lb. Fontina cheese, diced
3/4 cup milk
2 tbs. butter
3 egg yolks
1/4 tsp. white pepper
1 thinly sliced white truffle (optional)
buttered toast fingers or Italian breadsticks

Combine cheese and milk. Refrigerate for several hours to soften cheese.

18

When ready to prepare, transfer to a heavy saucepan. Cook over low heat, stirring constantly, about 5 minutes or until cheese melts. It may be somewhat stringy at this point. Beat yolks lightly. Gradually stir about 1/4 cup of hot cheese mixture into yolks. Pour slowly back into cheese mixture, beating constantly. Continue cooking over low heat until mixture becomes smooth and finally thickens. Add truffles. Serve Fonduta in chafing dish blazer pan over hot water. It is eaten by dipping toast fingers or Italian breadsticks into mixture. Makes 4 servings.

FONDUE WITH CHIVES

3 tbs. butter

3-1/2 tbs. chopped chives

1 cup dry white wine

1/2 lb. Swiss cheese, diced

1 tsp. flour

2 egg yolks, beaten

salt, pepper, nutmeg to taste

French or Italian bread, cubed

Melt butter in fondue pot over low heat. Lightly sauté chives. Pour in wine and heat. Toss cheese with flour. Add to wine and stir until melted. Stir 3 tablespoons hot cheese mixture into egg yolks. Slowly pour back into fondue pot, stirring constantly. Season and serve. Eat by spearing bread cubes on forks and dipping into mixture. Makes 3 to 4 servings.

CAERPHILLY FONDUE

1 clove garlic, cut in half

2 tbs. butter

2 tbs. flour

1-1/2 cups milk, warmed

2 cups (8 oz.) diced Caerphilly cheese

1/2 tsp. salt

pepper to taste

French or Italian bread, cubed

Rub chafing dish blazer pan with cut garlic. Add butter and melt over moderate heat. Stir in flour and let bubble. Place pan over hot water. Slowly stir in warm milk. Cook until mixture thickens, stirring occasionally. Add cheese and seasonings and stir until cheese is melted. Turn heat low and serve. Eat by spearing bread cubes on forks and dipping into mixture. Also, good spooned over toast or English muffins. Makes 4 servings.

SIMPLE SIMON FONDUE

1 garlic clove, cut in half
1 lb. diced cheddar or American cheese
1/2 cup milk
1 tsp. dry mustard

salt, cayenne, paprika to taste
1 egg, separated
French or Italian bread, cubed

Rub chafing dish blazer pan with cut garlic. Add cheese. Place pan over hot water pan. Stir cheese until melted. Combine milk, seasonings and beaten egg yolk. Blend into melted cheese. Cook until thickened. Carefully fold in stiffly beaten egg white and serve immediately. Eat by spearing bread cubes on forks and dipping into mixture. Makes 4 servings.

FONDUE A LA GEORGIANA

1 large loaf crusty French bread
1 garlic clove, cut in half
6 eggs
1 cup (4 oz.) grated Gruyère cheese

4 tbs. butter
pinch salt
freshly grated pepper
parsley

Cut bread into cubes with some crust on each cube. Rub fondue pot with cut clove of garlic. Beat eggs until whites and yolks are well mixed. Add cheese and butter. Put mixture into fondue pot. Place over low heat. Cook, stirring with a wooden spoon, until mixture begins to set but is still soft. Add very little salt but a good grating of pepper. Sprinkle with chopped parsley. Eat by spearing bread cubes on forks and dipping into mixture. Makes 4 servings.

FONDUE ROUGE

1-1/2 cups American cheese, coarsely grated
1/2 cup blue cheese
1 tsp. Worcestershire sauce
1/2 cup condensed tomato soup
2 tbs. sherry
French or Italian bread, cut into cubes

    Combine cheese, Worcestershire and soup in fondue pot. Stir constantly over low heat until cheese is melted and mixture is creamy. Add sherry and blend. Eat by spearing bread cubes on forks and dipping into mixture. Makes 4 servings.

CHEDDAR CHEESE FONDUE

1 tbs. dry mustard
2 tbs. water
3 tbs. butter
3 tbs. flour

pepper to taste
1 cup milk
2 cups (8 oz.) diced cheddar cheese
French or Italian bread cubes

Combine mustard and water. Let stand 15 minutes. Melt butter in saucepan over medium heat. Add flour and pepper. Cook 1 minute. Remove from heat. Slowly stir in milk. Return to heat and cook, stirring, until mixture boils. Add cheese. Stir until melted. Blend in mustard mixture. Transfer to fondue pot. Eat by spearing bread cubes on forks and dipping into mixture. Makes 4 servings.

CHEDDAR FONDUE WITH HORSERADISH

1/2 lb. cheddar cheese, diced

1 tbs. butter

1/3 cup milk, warmed

1 tsp. Worcestershire sauce

3/4 tsp. prepared horseradish

1/2 tsp. salt

pepper to taste

1 egg, separated

2 tbs. sherry

paprika

French or Italian bread, cubed

Melt cheese and butter in chafing dish blazer pan over hot water. Slowly stir in milk and seasonings. Blend in beaten egg yolk. Cook, stirring, a few minutes until thickened and smooth. Remove from heat. Fold in stiffly beaten egg white and sherry. Serve in chafing dish over hot water. Eat by spearing bread cubes on forks and dipping into mixture. Makes 4 servings.

CIDER FONDUE

1 tsp. flour

1 tsp. dry mustard

2 cups apple cider

2 lbs. aged cheddar cheese

2 tbs. butter

salt and pepper to taste

French or Italian bread, cubed

Mix flour and mustard together. Blend into 1/2 cup cider with a fork. Heat remaining cider in saucepan over low heat. Add cheese and butter. Stir constantly until smooth and cheese is melted. Add mustard mixture and seasonings. Pour into fondue pot and serve. Eat by spearing bread cubes on forks and dipping into mixture. Makes 8 servings.

CRAB MEAT FONDUE

1/2 cup butter

4 small onions, chopped

1 lb. cheddar cheese, diced

3/4 cup catsup

1/4 cup Worcestershire sauce

1/4 cup sherry

salt and pepper to taste

4 cups crab meat

French or Italian bread for dipping

    Melt butter in fondue pot or saucepan over low heat. Sauté onions until glazed, but not browned. Add cheese, catsup, Worcestershire sauce, sherry and seasonings. Stir constantly until mixture is smooth. Add crab meat. Serve in fondue pot or chafing dish over low heat. Eat by spearing bite-sized pieces of crusty bread on forks and dipping into mixture. Makes 6 servings.

LOBSTER FONDUE

1 lb. lobster meat
2 truffles (optional)
2 tbs. butter
2 tbs. sherry
salt, cayenne, paprika to taste
3 egg yolks, beaten
1 cup (1/2 pt.) cream

Cut lobster into 1-inch cubes and chop truffles. Melt butter in chafing dish blazer pan over low heat. Lightly sauté truffles. Add lobster, sherry and seasonings. Place over hot water. Mix egg yolks and cream. Combine with lobster mixture. Stir until heated. Makes 4 to 6 servings.

FONDUE MARSEILLAISE

2 cups milk

1 cup grated Swiss cheese

3 tbs. flour

1 tbs. Worcestershire sauce

1 tsp. salt

1/2 tsp. dry mustard

1 lb. cooked shrimp

Combine all ingredients except shrimp in a blender container. Cover and blend on high until everything is well combined. Pour into saucepan. Cook over medium heat, stirring constantly, until smooth and thickened. Serve in fondue pot. Eat by spearing shrimp on forks and dipping into mixture. Makes 4 servings.

BERNIE'S FONDUE

1/2 cup butter

1 onion, chopped

1/3 cup flour

1/2 cup cream

1/4 cup tomato paste

1/2 cup pureed chicken livers

2 tbs. Worcestershire sauce

salt and cayenne to taste

1/2 cup grated Parmesan cheese

1/2 cup Cognac

Melt butter in heavy saucepan over medium heat. Sauté onion. Add flour and stir 5 minutes. Add cream, tomato paste, chicken livers, Worcestershire, salt and cayenne. Reduce heat to low and cook 20 minutes, stirring frequently. Remove from heat. Stir in cheese until melted. Blend in Cognac. Serve in chafing dish. Makes 4 to 6 servings.

FONDUE AVEC OEUFS

6 hard-cooked eggs
3/4 cup bread crumbs
3 tbs. finely chopped parsley
2 tbs. finely chopped chives
1/4 tsp. dill weed
salt, cayenne, paprika
Fondue Chablis, page 11

Cut eggs in half lengthwise. Remove yolks and mash with bread crumbs and seasonings. Stuff egg whites with filling. Serve with fondue spooned over them. Makes 4 to 6 servings.

FONDUE BOURGUIGNONNE

Fondue Bourguignonne, according to legend, had its beginning centuries ago in the famous vineyards of the Burgundy region of France. During the harvest season the grapes had to be picked at the precise time of ripeness without even stopping to eat! Someone had the idea of keeping a pot of fat boiling so each worker could quickly cook his own pieces of meat in spare moments. The Swiss, famous for cheese fondue, developed the idea to its present form and honored its Burgundy origin by calling it Fondue Bourguignonne.

The right equipment for meat fondue is extremely important. Not just any kind of pot will do in this case. It has to be made of metal in order to stand the high heat and keep the fat hot while it's being used. And it must set securely on its stand to avoid the danger of tipping. The traditional fondue bourguignonne pot is wide at the base and narrow at the top. This shape helps to eliminate some of the spattering and hold in the heat. A tray beneath the pot will help catch some of the spatters and many fondue sets come with a tray.

The heat source, over which the fondue pot sets, must be adequate enough to keep the fat hot during the entire cooking process. Those which can be adjusted are best and butane or alcohol burners are preferable. Forks used for cooking should be a minimum of 10 inches in length with long tines for securing the food. Many have color-keyed handles or tips so each person can recognise his own. Special fondue plates with sections for the sauces are attractive and awfully nice to have. They come in a variety of styles.

Never have the pot more than half full of oil. And, unless your fondue pot is electric, it is better to heat the oil to the desired temperature on the range and then bring it to the table. The recommended temperature is about 375°F. Test with a deep fat thermometer or cubes of bread or meat. Bread will brown in about 60 seconds at that temperature and the oil will sizzle upon contact with the meat and it will start to brown immediately. Adjust heat source to keep the oil as close to that temperature during cooking as possible. A good quality of oil should always be used. For extra flavor, half oil and half clarified butter are sometimes used. Be careful to keep the temperature below 400°F or the clarified butter will begin to smoke.

For the best fondue use good cuts of high quality meat. Remove all fat, cut into bite-sized pieces and pat dry to cut down on spattering. Take the meat from the refrigerator about 30 minutes before using. It will cook faster and the oil can maintain its temperature easier if the meat is not cold.

Guests should be provided with dinner forks since fondue forks become extremely hot and seriously burned lips could result if they are used for eating.

Besides a variety of sauces, a crisp green salad, crusty French bread or rolls and glasses of wine is all that is needed to accompany any of the meat fondues. However, there are no set rules so you may serve any menu you like.

CLASSIC FONDUE BOURGUIGNONNE

2 lbs. beef filet or boneless sirloin
oil to half fill fondue pot
3 to 5 dipping sauces
salt and pepper

Trim all fat from meat. Cut into bite-sized pieces. Arrange on small plates so each guest may have his own. Heat oil in fondue pot to about 375° F. Place in center of table over heat source. Each guest spears a cube of meat on his fondue fork and cooks it to his liking (about 30 seconds for medium-rare). Remove meat from fondue fork and start another piece cooking. Season cooked meat and dip into sauces as desired. Makes 4 servings.

41

MIXED GRILL FONDUE

1/2 lb. beef filet or boneless sirloin
1/2 lb. lean pork
1/2 lb. veal cutlets, pounded
4 veal kidneys

4 chicken livers
oil to half fill fondue pot
3 to 5 sauces for dipping
salt and pepper

Trim all fat from meat. Cut into bite-sized pieces. Arrange several pieces of each meat on small plates for guests. Heat oil in fondue pot to about 375° F. Place in center of table over heat source. Each guest spears a cube of meat on his fondue fork and cooks it to his liking (about 30 seconds for medium-rare). Remove meat from fondue fork and start another piece cooking. Season cooked meat with salt and pepper and dip into sauces as desired. Makes about 4 servings.

CHICKEN OR TURKEY FONDUE

2 lbs. chicken or turkey breast meat
oil to half fill fondue pot
3 to 5 sauces for dipping
salt and pepper

   Cut raw breast meat into bite-sized pieces. Arrange on small plates so each guest has his own. Heat oil in fondue pot to about 375°F. Place in the center of the table over heat source. Each guest spears a cube of meat on his fondue fork and cooks it to his liking. Remove from fondue fork. Season with salt and pepper and dip into sauces. Makes 4 servings.

44

LAMB FONDUE

2 lbs. tender lamb
oil to half fill fondue pot
3 to 5 dipping sauces
salt and pepper

Ask your butcher for a tender cut. A small leg might be the best buy. Remove all fat from meat and cut into bite-sized pieces. Arrange on small plates so each guest may have his own. Heat oil in fondue pot to 375°F. Place in the center of the table over heat source. Each guest spears a cube of lamb on his fondue fork and cooks it to his liking. Remove from fondue fork. Season with salt and pepper and dip into sauce. Makes 4 servings.

PORK OR HAM FONDUE

2 lbs. lean pork or ham
oil to half fill fondue pot
3 to 5 sauces for dipping
salt and pepper

Cut meat into bite-sized pieces. Arrange on small plates so each guest will have his own. Heat oil in fondue pot to about 375°F. Place in the center of the table over heat source. Each guest spears a cube of meat on his fondue fork and cooks it to his liking. (Be sure pork is cooked well-done.) Remove meat from fondue fork. Season, if desired. Dip into sauce. Makes 4 servings.

SEAFOOD FONDUE

1/2 lb. salmon steaks

1/2 lb. other firm-fleshed fish

1/2 lb. medium-sized raw shrimp

1/2 lb. scallops

1/2 lb. rock lobster tails, shelled

oil to half fill fondue pot

3 to 5 sauces for dipping

Cut fish in 3/4-inch cubes. Peel and devein shrimp. Cut shallops and lobster into bite-sized pieces. Line a tray or platter with greens. Arrange seafood on greens. Heat oil to 375°F in fondue pot. Place in center of table over heat source. Spear seafood on fondue forks and cook in the hot oil about 1 minute. Remove cooked seafood from fondue fork and dip into sauces as desired. Makes 4 to 6 servings.

LOW CALORIE FONDUE

This version of fondue is very popular with calorie watchers. Meats and vegetables are cooked in this delicious broth instead of being deep fried. Broth may be substituted for oil in any of the previous recipes. After the meat has all been cooked, the flavorful broth can be served as a tasty bonus.

2-1/2 cups beef or chicken broth

1-1/4 cups water

1/2 cup dry white wine

1/2 bunch green onions, chopped

1 stalk celery, chopped

few sprigs parsley

salt and pepper

1 tsp. fines herbes

Simmer ingredients in saucepan 10 minutes. Remove from heat and let stand 2 hours. Strain into fondue pot and bring to boiling. Use as directed.

FONDUE BOURGUIGNONNE SAUCES

ANCHOVY SAUCE

1 cup mayonnaise

1 tbs. chopped parsley

1 tbs. capers, drained

1 tbs. chopped anchovies

1 hard-cooked egg, finely chopped

1 tsp. dry mustard

garlic powder to taste

Combine ingredients. Chill. Makes about 1-1/3 cups.

AVOCADO SAUCE

2 ripe avocados
2 tbs. minced onion
1 tbs. lemon juice
1 tbs. mayonnaise
2 drops Tabasco
salt to taste

Mash avocados. Stir in onion, lemon juice, mayonnaise, Tabasco and salt. Mix until well blended. Makes about 1-1/2 cups.

EASY BARBECUE SAUCE

1 bottle (12 oz.) extra-hot catsup
3 tbs. vinegar

2 tsp. celery seed
1 clove garlic, cut

Combine ingredients. Chill several hours. Remove garlic before serving. May also be served warm, if desired. Makes 1-1/4 cups.

SPICY CATSUP

3/4 cup catsup
2 tbs. vinegar

1/2 tsp. prepared horseradish

Combine ingredients. Chill. Makes about 3/4 cup.

QUICK AND EASY MUSHROOM SAUCE

2/3 cup catsup   1/4 tsp. Tabasco
2 tbs. canned mushrooms, chopped

Combine ingredients. Chill. Makes 3/4 cup.

SOUR CREAM HORSERADISH SAUCE

1 cup (1/2 pt.) sour cream   1/4 tsp. salt
3 tbs. prepared horseradish, well drained   dash paprika
1 tsp. lemon juice or vinegar

Combine all ingredients. Chill. Makes about 1-1/4 cups.

SOUR CREAM MUSTARD SAUCE

1 cup (1/2 pt.) sour cream   2 tbs. chopped green onions
3 tbs. prepared mustard   salt and pepper to taste

Mix ingredients together well. Chill. Makes about 1-1/4 cups.

CURRY MAYONNAISE

1/2 cup mayonnaise   1 tsp. lemon juice
1/2 cup sour cream   1 tsp. curry powder

Combine mayonnaise and sour cream. Blend in lemon juice and curry.
Taste. Add more seasoning if desired. Chill. Makes about 1 cup.

ROQUEFORT BUTTER

4 oz. Roquefort cheese   1 clove garlic, crushed
1/2 cup butter   3 drops bitters
1 tbs. prepared mustard

Blend ingredients together well. Serve at room temperature.

SOUR CREAM CHUTNEY SAUCE

3/4 cup sour cream   pinch curry powder
1/4 cup chutney

Combine ingredients and chill to blend flavors. Makes 1 cup.

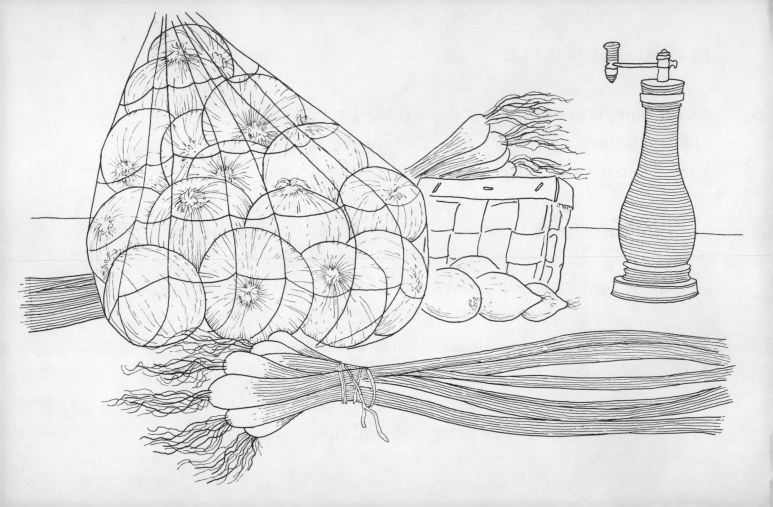

BLENDER BEARNAISE SAUCE

4 shallots
1/2 cup tarragon vinegar
2 egg yolks

salt, cayenne pepper
1 tsp. <u>each</u> parsley, chives, tarragon
1/2 cup melted butter, cooled

Place shallots and vinegar in blender container. Cover. Run on low speed 15 seconds or until shallots are chopped. Pour mixture into small saucepan. Reduce until it measures 2 tablespoons. Strain. Pour strained vinegar back into blender container. Add egg yolks, salt, cayenne, parsley, chives and tarragon. Cover. Blend on lowest speed. Remove cap (not cover) and gradually pour in cooled butter. Stop blending as soon as sauce thickens.

PIQUANT SAUCE FOR HAM

1/2 cup grape jelly   1-1/2 tsp. lemon juice
2 tbs. prepared mustard   1/8 tsp. cinnamon

Combine in a saucepan. Heat until jelly melts. Makes 2/3 cup.

TERIYAKI SAUCE

1/2 cup soy sauce   1/8 tsp. ground ginger
1 clove garlic, minced   1/4 cup sake or sherry
1 tbs. brown sugar

Combine ingredients. Makes about 3/4 cup.

TANGY MINT SAUCE FOR LAMB

1/2 cup mint jelly
2 tbs. butter
2 tbs. cider vinegar
1 tbs. lemon juice
1/2 tsp. dry mustard

Combine ingredients in small saucepan. Stir over low heat until jelly melts and mixture comes to a boil. Makes 3/4 cup.

TARTAR SAUCE

1/2 cup mayonnaise
1/2 cup sour cream
1 tbs. chopped stuffed olives
1 tbs. minced parsley
1 tbs. chopped capers
1 tbs. chopped sweet gerkins

   Combine mayonnaise and sour cream. Fold in remaining ingredients. Chill to blend flavors. Makes 1-1/4 cups.

CHINESE SWEET AND SOUR SAUCE

1/2 cup orange juice

1/2 cup pineapple juice

1/2 cup tomato paste

1 cup malt vinegar

1 cup sugar

1-1/2 tbs. salt

Combine ingredients in a heavy saucepan. (Use the amount of salt indicated, it will not be too much.) Bring mixture slowly to boil. Simmer 10 minutes. Prepare a thickening using 1 part cornstarch to 3 parts water. Slowly stir into sauce. Cook until thickened and clear. Store sauce in a wide-mouthed jar, loosely covered. It will keep for months in a cool dark place. Do not refrigerate as condensation will occur and a mold will form. And, if jar is tightly covered, acid gases will accumulate inside of the jar causing spoilage. Makes about 3-1/2 cups.

DESSERT FONDUE

A dessert fondue will top off any meal with a special feeling of fellowship. Into these tasty blends of chocolate and other confections dip chunks of angel food cake, lady fingers, pound cake, or bite-size cream puff pastry. Fresh fruits - strawberries, grapes, bananas, pears or papayas - are also delicious. Canned fruit may also be used. Be sure to drain well. A little bit of care and imagination in arranging will make any of these dessert fondues a colorful and unusual way to finish a meal.

FONDUE AU CHOCOLAT

Chocolate fondue is actually an American invention. It is said to have originated in a New York restaurant. There are many variations of the basic recipe.

9 oz. Swiss chocolate, broken into pieces
1/2 cup whipping cream

Combine ingredients in a fondue pot or chafing dish. Stir over very low heat until chocolate is melted and the mixture is smooth. Eat by spearing cubes of cake, marshmallows or pieces of fruit on forks and dipping into mixture. Makes 6 servings.

VARIATIONS OF FONDUE AU CHOCOLAT

Use bittersweet chocolate instead of milk chocolate.

Use pretzels of various shapes for dipping.

Add any one of the following to the Fondue Au Chocolate recipe:

— 1/2 cup crushed almonds

— 2 tablespoons kirsch

— 1 tablespoon instant coffee

— 1/4 teaspoon ground cinnamon and 1/4 teaspoon ground cloves

— mint flavoring

FONDUE AU CREME

1 cup powdered sugar
1 cup heavy cream

Combine sugar and cream in saucepan. Bring to boil, stirring constantly. Boil about half a minute. Pour into fondue pot or chafing dish. Keep heat as low as possible to prevent scorching. Flavorings such as vanilla, almond or lemon may be added. Serve by spearing pieces of cake or fruit on forks and dipping into mixture. Makes 4 servings.

CHEDDAR CHEESE FONDUE WITH APPLES

3 tbs. butter
3 tbs. flour
1 cup milk
2 cups (8 oz.) diced sharp, cheddar cheese
crisp, green apples

Melt butter in fondue pot over medium heat. Stir in flour. Let bubble a minute. Remove from heat. Slowly stir in milk. Return to heat and cook, stirring, until mixture thickens and boils. Add diced cheese. Stir until melted and smooth. Eat by spearing bite-size chunks of crisp, green apples on forks and dipping into mixture. Makes 6 servings.

BAKED FONDUES

Although baked fondues are not as spectacular as souffles they do have a similar texture and are sometimes thought of as simplified souffles. Happily the fear of having a beautiful souffle collapse on its way to the table doesn't exist with its country cousin, which originated many years ago as a practical way of using stale bread or bread crumbs. Many variations of this nutritious and economical discovery have appeared over the years and they still are one of our favorite make-ahead party dishes. Baked fondues with meat or fish are perfect main course dishes and lend themselves beautifully to buffet suppers. They require very little else to make a delicious company meal.

A lovely buffet supper might consist of a baked main dish fondue, your favorite tossed salad, a pretty molded salad, buttered vegetable, crusty rolls, cake and a beverage --- most of which can easily be prepared in advance.

EASY CHEESE FONDUE

1 cup bread crumbs
1 cup milk, warmed
1 cup (4 oz.) grated cheese
2 tbs. melted butter
salt, cayenne pepper to taste
1 egg, separated

Soak bread crumbs in milk. Stir in cheese, butter, salt and cayenne. Add beaten egg yolk. Fold in stiffly beaten egg white. Pour mixture into well-buttered casserole. Sprinkle with extra grated cheese, if desired. Bake in 325°F oven 1 hour, or until knife inserted in center comes out clean. Makes 2 servings.

CHEDDAR CHEESE FONDUE

soft butter
8 slices bread
1-3/4 lbs. sharp cheddar, grated
6 eggs
2-1/2 cups half & half
1 tbs. minced onion

1 tsp. brown sugar
1/2 tsp. Beau Monde seasoning
1/2 tsp. Worcestershire sauce
1/2 tsp. dry mustard
salt, pepper to taste

Butter bread and dice. Scatter half of bread cubes on the bottom of a buttered casserole dish. Add half of the cheese, then another layer of bread and top with remaining cheese. Beat eggs. Blend with remaining ingredients. Pour over cheese. Refrigerate for 1 hour. Bake in 300°F oven about 1 hour, or until knife inserted in center comes out clean. Makes 6 servings.

FONDUE MARIA

1 clove garlic, cut in half
1 cup milk, warmed
1 cup bread crumbs
1 cup (4 oz.) diced cheese

1 tbs. butter
salt, cayenne, paprika to taste
3 eggs, separated

Rub bottom and sides of a casserole dish with cut garlic, then butter it well. Combine milk, crumbs, cheese, butter and seasonings in a heavy saucepan. Cook over medium heat until cheese melts and mixture is smooth. Remove from heat. Stir in beaten egg yolks. Fold in stiffly beaten egg whites. Pour into prepared casserole. Bake in 350°F oven 35 to 40 minutes, or until knife inserted in center comes out clean. Makes 4 servings.

PETITE FONDUES

1 cup bread crumbs
2 cups milk
2 eggs, beaten
1/2 lb. cheese, grated
1 tbs. melted butter
salt and pepper to taste

    Combine bread crumbs and milk. Add eggs, cheese, melted butter and seasonings. Pour into buttered individual ramekins or casserole dish. Sprinkle more crumbs on top if desired. Bake in 300°F oven 1 hour, or until knife inserted in center comes out clean. Makes 6 servings.

FONDUE FOR TWO

1 cup bread crumbs
1 cup milk, warmed
1 cup (4 oz.) grated cheese
2 tbs. butter
salt and cayenne to taste
1 egg, separated

Soak bread crumbs in milk. Add cheese, butter, salt and cayenne. Beat egg yolk until creamy. Stir into cheese mixture. Fold in stiffly beaten egg white. Pour into well-buttered casserole. Put extra cheese on top, if desired. Bake in 325°F oven 1 hour, or until knife inserted in center comes out clean. Makes 2 servings.

FONDUE WITH BEER

8 slices bread, buttered
8 slices American cheese
3 eggs, beaten
1 tsp. Worcestershire sauce
1/2 tsp. dry mustard
1 cup beer

Make 4 sandwiches using buttered bread and four slices cheese. Place in buttered baking dish. Top with remaining cheese slices. Beat eggs and seasonings together. Stir in beer. Pour over sandwiches. Bake in 350°F oven about 40 minutes, or until set. Makes 4 servings.

CHEDDAR AND BEER FONDUE

1 cup milk

2 tbs. chopped onion

1 cup beer

3 cups (12 oz.) grated cheddar cheese

2-1/2 cups bread cubes

1 tsp. salt

1/2 tsp. dry mustard

4 eggs, separated

2 tbs. butter

2 tsp. caraway seeds

Combine milk and onion in saucepan. Scald over low heat. Add beer, cheese, 2 cups bread cubes, salt and dry mustard. Stir until cheese melts. Lightly beat egg yolks. Slowly add to mixture, stirring constantly. Fold in stiffly beaten egg whites. Pour into well buttered casserole. Dot with butter. Sprinkle with caraway seeds and remaining 1/2 cup bread cubes. Bake in 325° F oven 1-1/4 hours. Makes 6 servings.

PARISIAN FONDUE

1-1/2 loaves French bread, sliced
1/2 cup soft butter
1/2 cup prepared mustard
1-1/2 lbs. sliced cheddar cheese

4 eggs, beaten
5 cups milk, heated
1-1/2 tsp. Worcestershire sauce
salt, cayenne, paprika to taste

Spread bread slices with butter and mustard. Cover bottom of large, well-buttered casserole with slices of bread. Cover bread with cheese slices. Continue until bread and cheese are all used, ending with bread. Combine eggs, hot milk, Worcestershire sauce and seasonings. Pour over bread. Refrigerate several hours or overnight. Bake in 350°F oven 1-1/2 hours, or until knife inserted in center comes out clean. Makes 8 servings.

CRAB MEAT FONDUE

2 cups milk

1/4 cup butter

1-3/4 cups bread crumbs

1 clove garlic, minced

1/2 tsp. minced onion

1/2 tsp. salt

1/4 tsp. ground ginger

pepper to taste

5 eggs, separated

1 cup (4 oz.) grated cheddar cheese

1 can (7 oz.) flaked crab meat

Heat milk in saucepan. Add butter, bread crumbs, garlic, minced onion, salt, ginger and pepper. Add beaten egg yolks. Cook, stirring constantly, over low heat until thickened. Stir in cheese and crab meat. Fold in stiffly beaten egg whites. Pour into well-buttered casserole. Bake in 325°F oven 1-1/2 hours, or until knife inserted in center comes out clean. Makes 4 servings.

LA FONDUE HESTERE

1 can (7 oz.) tuna

1 cup chopped celery

1/4 cup mayonnaise

1 tbs. dry mustard

1/2 tsp. salt

12 slices bread

6 slices cheddar cheese

3 eggs, beaten

2-1/2 cups milk

2 tsp. Worcestershire sauce

Combine tuna, celery, mayonnaise, mustard and salt. Trim crusts from bread. Spread tuna mixture on 6 slices of bread. Cover with remaining bread. Place sandwiches in buttered baking dish. Top with cheese slices. Combine eggs, milk and Worcestershire sauce. Pour over sandwiches. Bake in 325°F oven about 45 minutes, or until knife inserted in center comes out clean. Makes 6 servings.

NEW ORLEANS FONDUE

1 can (8 oz.) salmon

1 cup minced celery

1/4 cup mayonnaise

1 tbs. dry mustard

1/4 tsp. salt

12 slices bread

6 slices American cheese

3 eggs, beaten

2-1/2 cups milk

2 tsp. Worcestershire sauce

Drain and flake salmon. Discard skin and bones. Combine salmon, celery, mayonnaise, mustard and salt. Trim crusts from bread. Spread salmon mixture on 6 slices of bread. Cover with remaining bread. Place sandwiches in buttered baking dish. Top with cheese slices. Combine eggs, milk and Worcestershire. Pour over sandwiches. Bake in 325°F oven 45 minutes, or until knife inserted in center comes out clean. Makes 6 servings.

CHICKEN FONDUE

4 eggs, separated
1 can (10-1/2 oz.) cream of chicken soup
1-1/2 cups diced, cooked chicken
1 cup grated cheddar cheese
2 cups bread crumbs
salt, cayenne, paprika to taste

Beat egg yolks until light. Add soup, chicken, cheese, bread crumbs and seasonings. Fold in stiffly beaten egg whites. Pour into well-buttered casserole dish. Bake in 325°F oven 1 hour, or until knife inserted in center comes out clean. Makes 4 servings.

TURKEY FONDUE

1 cup milk

1 cup turkey stock

2 tbs. butter

1-3/4 cups bread crumbs

2 tbs. lemon juice

1 tsp. ground thyme

1/4 tsp. salt

1/4 tsp. freshly ground pepper

5 eggs, separated

2 cups diced turkey

Heat milk, stock and butter in heavy saucepan over medium heat. Add bread crumbs, lemon juice, thyme, salt and pepper. Stir in beaten egg yolks. Cook, stirring constantly, until thickened. Stir in turkey. Remove from heat. Fold in stiffly beaten egg whites. Turn into well-buttered casserole. Bake in a pan of hot water, in 325°F oven, 1-1/4 hours, or until knife inserted in center comes out clean. Makes 4 servings.

FONDUE NOEL

1-1/2 lbs. pork sausage
2 tbs. minced green onions
1/4 cup chopped pimiento
1 tsp. dry mustard
salt and pepper to taste

12 slices bread
6 eggs, beaten
3 cups milk
2 tsp. Worcestershire sauce

Sauté sausage. Drain off fat. Stir in onion, pimiento, mustard, salt and pepper. Trim crusts from bread. Line a buttered baking dish with 6 slices of bread. Cover with sausage mixture. Top with remaining bread slices. Combine eggs, milk and Worcestershire sauce. Pour over bread. Bake in 325°F oven 1-1/2 hours, or until set. Makes 6 servings.

84

RICE FONDUE

4 eggs, separated
1-1/2 cups milk
2 cups (8 oz.) grated sharp cheddar cheese
2 cups coooked rice
1 tsp. salt
pepper to taste

Beat egg yolks well. Add milk, cheese, rice and seasonings. Mix well. Beat egg white until stiff, but not dry. Fold into rice mixture. Pour into buttered casserole. Bake in pan of hot water, in 350°F oven, 1 hour, or until knife inserted in center comes out clean. Makes 6 servings.

ASPARAGUS FONDUE

3 slices bread, cubed

1 pkg. (10 oz.) frozen asparagus, thawed

3/4 cup (6 oz.) grated cheese

1 egg, beaten

1 cup milk

1 tbs. butter, melted

1 tsp. minced onion

1/2 tsp. salt

pepper to taste

Arrange layers of bread cubes, asparagus and 1/2 cup cheese in buttered casserole. Blend together egg, milk, butter, onion, salt and pepper. Pour over casserole ingredients. Sprinkle with remaining cheese. Bake in 350°F oven 45 minutes, or until knife inserted in center comes out clean. Makes 4 servings.

CORN AND CHEESE FONDUE

1 cup milk
1 cup canned corn
1 cup grated American cheese
1-1/2 cups bread crumbs
1 tbs. butter, melted
salt, pepper, paprika to taste
3 eggs, separated

Combine milk, corn, cheese, bread crumbs, butter and seasonings. Add beaten egg yolks. Fold in stiffly beaten egg whites. Bake in well-buttered casserole in 350°F oven 1 hour, or until knife inserted in center comes out clean. Makes 4 servings.

LEEK FONDUE

soft butter
6 slices bread
1-1/2 cups (6 oz.) grated cheddar cheese
3 eggs, well beaten
3 cups milk

2 tbs. diced leeks
3/4 tsp. dry mustard
3/4 tsp. salt
pepper to taste

Butter bread and cut into cubes. Place in buttered baking dish. Spread cheese evenly over bread cubes. Combine remaining ingredients. Pour over bread. Let stand 2 hours. Bake in 350°F oven 40 minutes, or until a knife inserted in the center comes out clean. Makes 6 servings.

PARMESAN FONDUE

2 tbs. butter	3 eggs, separated
1 tbs. flour	4 oz. grated Parmesan cheese
1/2 cup milk	salt, pepper, cayenne to taste

Melt butter in heavy saucepan over medium heat. Stir in flour and allow to bubble a minute or two. Remove from heat. Gradually add milk. Return to heat and cook, stirring, until thickened. Beat in egg yolks and seasonings. Stir in Parmesan until melted. Beat egg whites until stiff, but not dry. Fold into cheese mixture. Turn mixture into well-buttered casserole or baking dish. Bake in 350°F oven 1 hour or until firm in center. Makes 4 servings.

SPINACH FONDUE

1-1/3 cups milk, warmed
1-1/3 cups bread crumbs
1/2 tsp. salt
1/4 cup melted butter

4 eggs, separated
1 cup cooked, chopped spinach
2/3 cup American cheese

Combine milk and bread crumbs in top of double boiler. Let stand 5 minutes. Add salt and melted butter. Beat egg yolks and blend into crumb mixture. Cook over hot water until thickened. Cool. Add well-drained spinach and cheese to cooled mixture. Fold in stiffly beaten egg whites. Pour into buttered casserole. Bake in pan of hot water, in 350°F oven 1 hour, or until knife inserted in center comes out clean. Makes 4 servings.

RAREBITS

In recent years there has been a difference of opinion regarding the name of this delicious concoction. Some call it rarebit while others prefer rabbit. Because the name rabbit already belongs to something else, rarebit seems to be the popular choice.

A rarebit as it is prepared today is quite similar to fondue. Originally, the bread was toasted, soaked in wine, then covered with cheese, and toasted again. The result was similar to a grilled sandwich. Today the cheese is melted, as with fondue, and served over toasted bread. There is no reason why, if you so desire, you couldn't dip the bread in the rarebit instead. How ever you serve it, you will surely agree that it is a rare bit of eating pleasure, especially nice in the winter for an after-the-theatre supper, a brunch or as a snack with crackers for a large crowd.

QUICK WELSH RAREBIT

1 tbs. butter

2 lbs. American or cheddar cheese, diced

1 tbs. grated onion

1 tsp. Worcestershire sauce

1/2 tsp. dry mustard

1/2 tsp. salt

pepper and paprika to taste

1 cup ale

Melt butter and cheese in top of double boiler over hot water, stirring constantly. Add remaining ingredients. Cook, stirring, until mixture is smooth. Serve in chafing dish or fondue pot with French bread for dipping, or spoon over toast. Makes 6 to 8 servings.

LONDON RAREBIT

3 tbs. butter

3 tbs. flour

1/2 tsp. salt

dash Tabasco sauce

1/2 cup milk

1-1/2 cup (6 oz.) diced cheddar cheese

1/4 cup sherry

1 cup ale

Melt butter in saucepan over low heat. Stir in flour and seasonings. Let bubble a minute. Remove from heat. Slowly add milk. Cook over low heat, stirring constantly, until thickened. Add cheese and sherry. Stir until cheese is melted. Blend in ale. Serve in chafing dish or fondue pot with French bread for dipping, or spoon over toast. Makes 4 servings.

SPANISH RAREBIT

3 tbs. butter

2 green peppers, chopped

1/2 cup chopped onion

1 clove garlic, crushed

2 cups (8 oz.) grated American cheese

1 cup beer

1/4 tsp. Tabasco sauce

Melt butter in saucepan or chafing dish. Sauté pepper, onion and garlic 5 minutes. Slowly add cheese, stirring constantly until melted and smooth. Blend in beer and Tabasco sauce. Serve in chafing dish or fondue pot with French bread for dipping, or spoon over toast. Makes 4 servings.

SHERRY RAREBIT

1/3 cup cream
1 lb. American cheese, cubed
1/3 cup sherry
1/2 tsp. Worcestershire sauce
1 tsp. dry mustard

Combine cream and cheese in top of double boiler. Cook over hot water until cheese is melted and mixture is smooth. Add Worcestershire and mustard. Stir to blend. Serve in chafing dish or fondue pot with French bread for dipping, or spoon over toast. Makes 4 servings.

ROSY RAREBIT

1 can (8 oz.) tomatoes
1-1/2 tbs. butter
1 lb. American cheese, diced
salt and pepper to taste

    Drain tomatoes. Melt butter in heavy saucepan over low heat. Add drained tomatoes and simmer 20 minutes. Slowly add cheese, stirring constantly until it is melted and mixture has thickened. Season to taste. Serve over toast, or in chafing dish or fondue pot with French bread for dipping. Makes 4 servings.

RAREBIT A LA CREME

2 tbs. butter
1/2 lb. American or cheddar cheese, diced
1 egg, beaten
1/2 cup heavy cream
1/4 tsp. salt
pinch dry mustard
dash chili powder

Melt butter and cheese in heavy saucepan or chafing dish over low heat. Combine egg, cream and seasonings. Slowly blend into melted cheese. Stir until smooth and thickened. Serve over toast, or in a fondue pot or chafing dish with French bread for dipping. Makes 4 servings.

CREAM OF CELERY RAREBIT

1 can (10 oz.) cream of celery soup
1/4 cup dry white wine
1/2 tsp. mustard
1/2 tsp. Worcestershire sauce
1-1/2 cups (6 oz.) diced cheddar cheese
1 egg, well beaten

Combine soup, wine, mustard and Worcestershire in saucepan or chafing dish. Cook over medium heat until mixture is just beginning to boil. Slowly add cheese, stirring constantly until melted. Blend in well beaten egg and continue cooking until mixture reaches desired consistency. Serve with French bread for dipping, or spoon over toast. Makes 6 servings.

EASTERN-STYLE RAREBIT

Sherry Rarebit, page 97
1 can (4 oz.) sardines
1 tbs. butter
salt and pepper to taste
toasted English muffin halves

Prepare rarebit according to directions. Remove bones from sardines. Melt butter in frying pan. Gently sauté sardines about 10 minutes. Using a pancake turner or spatula, lay sauteed sardines on toasted muffin halves. Spoon Sherry Rarebit over sardines. Makes 4 to 6 servings.

WESTERN RAREBIT

1 jar (4 to 5 oz.) dried beef

2 tbs. butter

2 tbs. flour

1-1/2 cups milk

1 pkg. (4 oz.) sliced pimiento cheese, diced

2 eggs, beaten

pepper to taste

Shred beef and rinse with boiling water. Drain well. Melt butter in heavy saucepan over medium heat. Add flour and blend. Let bubble a minute or two. Remove from heat. Slowly stir in milk. Cook, stirring until thickened. Add cheese. Stir until melted. Mix a little of the hot mixture with the beaten eggs. Stir back into cheese sauce. Add beef and pepper. Cook, stirring, until thoroughly heated. Serve over toast. Makes 4 servings.

SPICY RAREBIT

1 tbs. butter

1 lb. cheddar cheese, diced

1 tbs. chili sauce

1 tsp. Tabasco sauce

1/2 tsp. mustard

salt and pepper to taste

6 or 7 tbs. ale

Melt butter in a heavy saucepan or chafing dish over low heat. Slowly add cheese and stir until melted. Blend in chili sauce, Tabasco, mustard and seasonings. Add ale, little by little. Cook, stirring constantly, until mixture is thickened and smooth. Serve in chafing dish or fondue pot with French bread for dipping, or spoon over toast. Makes 4 servings.

RED AND GREEN RAREBIT

1 lb. American cheese, diced
1 tsp. mustard
salt, cayenne and paprika to taste
1/2 cup ale
1 tbs. chopped green pepper
1 tbs. chopped pimiento

Melt cheese in heavy saucepan over low heat. Stir until smooth. Add mustard, salt, cayenne and paprika. Slowly blend in ale. Add pepper and pimiento. Serve in chafing dish or fondue pot with French bread for dipping, or spoon over toast. Makes 6 servings.

BEAN RAREBIT

2 tbs. butter

2/3 cup (about 3 oz.) grated cheddar cheese

1 cup baked beans with tomato sauce, mashed

1 tsp. Worcestershire sauce

1 tsp. salt

1/4 tsp. paprika

1 cup milk

Melt butter in saucepan over low heat. Slowly add cheese, stirring constantly until melted. Add beans and seasonings. Stir until mixture is blended and creamy. Add milk, a little at a time. Cook, stirring, until mixture reaches desired consistency. Serve in chafing dish or fondue pot with French bread for dipping, or spoon over toast. Makes 4 servings.

FRANKFURTER RAREBIT

2 tbs. butter
6 frankfurters
2 cups (8 oz.) shredded American cheese

3/4 cup milk
6 slices buttered toast
1 mild onion, sliced

Melt butter in frying pan over medium heat. Sauté frankfurters 15 minutes. Combine cheese and milk in top of double boiler. Cook over hot water, stirring constantly, until cheese melts and mixture is smooth. Slit frankfruters lengthwise, without cutting all the way through. Place, cut sides down, on toast slices. Spoon cheese mixture over franks and garnish with onion slices. Makes 6 servings.

CALIFORNIA SHRIMP RAREBIT

1 can (10 oz.) cream of shrimp soup
1 lb. cheddar cheese, diced
1/4 cup California sherry
salt and pepper to taste

Empty soup into top of double boiler. Add cheese. Place over hot water and stir until cheese is melted. Slowly blend in sherry and seasonings. Cook, stirring, until mixture reaches desired consistency. Serve in fondue pot or chafing dish with French bread for dipping, or spoon over toast. Makes 4 servings.

TUNA RAREBIT

1 tbs. butter

1 tbs. cheddar cheese, diced

1 tbs. minced onion

1 tsp. Worcestershire sauce

1 cup ale

1/2 tsp. dry mustard

1/2 tsp. salt

pepper and paprika to taste

1 cup (6-1/2 to 7 oz.) tuna

Melt butter and cheese together in the top of a double boiler over hot water. Stir constantly until mixture is smooth. Add onion, Worcestershire, ale, mustard, salt, pepper, paprika and tuna. Stir until heated and thickened. Serve in chafing dish or fondue pot with French bread for dipping, or spoon over toast. Makes 6 servings.

INDEX

110

MEAT FONDUE SAUCES

DESSERT FONDUE

RAREBITS

 NOTES

NOTES